Wales Coast Path: Pembrokeshire North

GW00649782

Text: *Dennis Kelsall*
Series editor: *Tony Bowerman*
Photographs: *Dennis Kelsall, © Crown copyright (2015) Visit Wales, David Evans/ Pembrokeshire Coastal Photography/www. pemcoastphotos.com, Drew Buckley/ www. drewbuckleyphotography.com, Vivienne Crow, Tony Bowerman, Dreamstime, Shutterstock*

Design: *Carl Rogers*

Northern Eye Books

ISBN 978-1-908632-29-6

A CIP catalogue record for this book is available from the British Library.

Cover: *Solva (Walk 10)*

Important Advice: The routes described in this book are undertaken at the reader's own risk. Walkers should take into account their level of fitness, wear suitable footwear and clothing, and carry food and water. It is also advisable to take the relevant OS map with you in case you get lost and leave the area covered by our maps.

Whilst every care has been taken to ensure the accuracy of the route directions, the publishers cannot accept responsibility for errors or omissions, or for changes in the details given. Nor can the publisher and copyright owners accept responsibility for any consequences arising from the use of this book.

If you find any inaccuracies in either the text or maps, please either write to us or email us at the addresses below. Thank you.

First published in 2015 by
Northern Eye Books Limited
Northern Eye Books, Tattenhall, Cheshire CH3 9PX
Email: tony@northerneyebooks.com

For sales enquiries, please call 01928 723 744

www.walescoastpath.co.uk
www.northerneyebooks.co.uk
www.top10walks.co.uk

 Twitter: @WalesCoastUK
@Northerneyeboo
@Top10walks

Contents

Britain's Only Coastal National Park

Although several of Britain's National Parks have a seaward boundary, only the Pembrokeshire park was specifically created to protect the coast. Facing the Atlantic, its coastline runs for 200 miles around the westernmost tip of Wales. The Pembrokeshire coast is a place of haunting beauty and perpetual contrast.

In places, a wild and untamed landscape faces the full fury of ocean storms, while elsewhere, craggy-cliffed headlands and fractured promontories protect coves and deep inlets backed by lush woodland. The rocks from which it is formed span more than 700 million years and few places in Britain possess such a concentration of dramatic geological features. Nature and a rich human heritage come together in a backdrop of stunning and ever-changing scenery, in which a profusion of wildflowers, birds and wildlife exploits the diversity of natural habitats.

The last rays of the setting sun dapple the grasses on Strumble Head

North Pembrokeshire Coast

Pembrokeshire's north coast has a rugged and remote quality, reflecting the wildness of the hills that rise behind. It was largely ignored during the Norman colonisation and even today beyond St Dogmael's there are only a handful of coastal communities. Yet burial cairns, promontory forts and a prehistoric trackway across the Preseli Hills indicate widespread prehistoric settlement, and it was an important focus during the spread of Celtic Christianity. Fishing, farming and stock grazing were traditional ways of life, but the Industrial Revolution briefly opened coastal quarrying and the railway made Fishguard an important Irish port. Today, it is a relative backwater but the coast has an untamed beauty, its flowers, birds, seals and porpoises making it a truly special place.

"I sense the mystery, infinity,
and love the space, the sea, in Pembrokeshire."

From *Ghazal of Pembrokeshire*, Pat Appleby, 2013

TOP 10 Walks: Pembrokeshire North

WHILE ALMOST EVERY BIT OF THE PEMBROKESHIRE COAST is worthy of inclusion, the ten walks selected here reflect its ever-changing character: from popular beaches to wild and rugged cliffs where soaring seabirds might be your only company. Almost all are circular, but can be extended there-and-back to include more of the coast, or you might take advantage of the excellent buses that service all the main access points along the Pembrokeshire stretch of the Wales Coast Path. It's superb coastal walking.

Newport Bay page 8

Dinas Island page 14

Goodwick & Carregwastad page 18

Strumble Head page 24

Looking across Newport beach at low tide

Newport Bay

Pembrokeshire's coastal bus service allows this one-way walk along a fine stretch of cliff above stacks and bays

What to expect:
Rugged clifftop paths with several ups and downs

Distance/time: 6.5km/ 4 miles. Allow 1½ to 2 hours

Start: Park at Pwllgwaelod and take the 'Poppit Rocket' to Newport Parrog (summer service only)

Grid refs: SN 004 399 (Pwllgwaelod), SN 051 396 (Parrog car park)

Ordnance Survey Map: OS Explorer OL35 (North Pembrokeshire)

After the walk: The Old Sailors pub/restaurant, Pwllgwaelod
SA42 0AE | 01348 811491

Walk outline

The short bus journey from Pwllgwaelod to Newport Parrog gives no hint of the coast's stunning scenery. The walking begins above the shoreline of the Nevern estuary, although at high tide a short detour might be necessary. Beyond Parrog's old lifeboat station, the path runs above a succession of bays to Cwm-yr-Eglwys. You can then either short cut behind Dinas Island or climb around the promontory (see Walk 2) back to Pwllgwaelod.

Deserted cliffs

Without Pembrokeshire's coastal bus service, many of the most impressive stretches of its coast are not readily accessible to the day walker, but this walk shows what is possible with a little planning. Often deserted, the cliffs west of Newport look down on inaccessible bays, where low tide reveals extensive rocky aprons planed flat by the waves. In contrast are the fine beaches at Aber Rhugian and Aber Fforest, where storms have piled shingle banks that pool the streams flowing from the deep valleys behind. At Cwm-yr-Eglwys, however, the sea is eroding the coast and has already claimed part of its tiny church.

Cwm-yr-Eglwys

Sea pinks or 'thrift'

The Walk

1. If you've come by car, park at **Pwllgwaelod** and take the **'Poppit Rocket' bus to Newport**, alighting at the **Parrog car park**.

Founded towards the end of the 12th century, Newport is one of the few Norman towns in North Pembrokeshire. Overseen by a castle sited on the flanks of Carningli, it was the seat of the Lords of Cemais and flourished as a centre for local industry and coastal trade. Quarries beneath the cliffs towards Cat Rock were worked for slate, while water-powered mills produced flannel from fleeces off the backs of hardy hill sheep. Small fishing boats and traders could moor alongside the dry-stone quay, but larger vessels had to go aground on the sands and wait for their cargoes

to be shifted by horse and cart at low tide, a practice that continued until the Second World War. The port had several warehouses, one of which survives as Newport Boat Club's headquarters.

2. Walk to the end of the street by the **Morawelon café** to pick up a path above the beach. Beyond seafront cottages, the way drops briefly along the shore to the next **slipway**. If it is covered at high tide, take the short, waymarked **Wales Coast Path diversion** to the left. Continue with the seafront path past more cottages into a tiny cove below the **old Parrog lifeboat station**, now a private house.

The small lifeboat station was built in 1884 but, although sheltered in a tiny cove, was poorly sited. Bad weather launches were hampered by strong tidal currents funnelled by the sand bar that all but

Summer scene: *The broad sands of Newport North Beach seen from the Parrog*

blocks the estuary, while at low tide, it was left high and dry. The station was abandoned after only 11 years and cover provided instead by the boat at Fishguard

3. Beyond the lifeboat station, take the higher path, which climbs onto **Carreg Germain**, a viewpoint overlooking the estuary and Newport Sands. Carry on above a succession of dramatic but inaccessible coves, divided by craggy headlands and a chaos of wave-worn stacks, the largest of which is **Cat Rock**. Eventually, the way turns in above

Sheltered bay?: *The ruins of St Brynach's church in front of cottages at Cwm-yr-Eglwys*

a deep, square-cut bay, dropping steeply through oak and hazel to a sturdy **wooden bridge** spanning **Aber Rhigian**. Turn towards the beach, passing a pool bunded by a broad shingle bank thrown up behind the beach.

4. Cross the beachhead and climb back onto the cliffs. The ongoing path winds in and out around deeply fractured promontories bracketing **Aber Ysgol**, where low tide exposes an extensive platform, planed flat by the relentless pounding of boulders moved back and forth by the waves. At the head of the next bay, **Aber Fforest**, the path descends more easily, passing behind a **lime kiln** to the beach.

5. Cross a bridge spanning the river and take the right fork, zig-zagging away through woodland. Breaking from the trees, look back for an inspiring prospect back to the bay before turning the point where a short, steep climb leads onto the top. Eventually, the views are lost as high hedges enclose the path. Beyond a gate, the path begins to fall, ultimately emerging past a farmhouse onto a lane. Head downhill to **Cwm-yr-Eglwys**.

Walk 1 – **Newport Bay** ♦ 13

6. If you're still hungry for spectacular cliff scenery, you can extend the walk over **Dinas Head**; follow the instructions given in Walk (**2**). Otherwise the return is across the valley that divides the rocky outcrop from the mainland. In which case, walk ahead into a car park and bear left to a gate. A path leads across open grass to a second gate and continues along the base of the wooded fold to Pwllgwaelod to complete the walk. ♦

Neolithic burial chambers

Nearby are two impressive Neolithic cromlechs built around 5,500 years ago. Carreg Coetan at Pen-y-Bont lies roughly 800 metres east of Parrog along the Coast Path; the burial chamber consists of an impressive capstone above four uprights. The second monument lies some 3½ miles to the south east at Pentre Ifan. This impressive, much photographed tomb is larger still and flanked by stones that formed a grand ceremonial entrance.

Cwm-yr-Eglwys bay seen from the eastern flanks of Dinas Island

Dinas Island

A short but strenuous walk onto Dinas Head, giving exhilarating views to the Preseli Hills and the coast

What to expect:
Good, low-level paths with a steep and rugged climb onto the top of the head

Distance/time: 5km/ 3 miles. Allow 1½ to 2 hours

Start: Cwm-yr-Eglwys

Grid ref: SN 004 400

Ordnance Survey Map: OS xplorer OL35 (North Pembrokeshire)

After the walk: The Old Sailors pub/restaurant, Pwllgwaelod SA42 0AE | 01348 811491

Walk outline

Leaving the tiny hamlet of Cwm-yr-Eglwys, the walk begins with a steady climb above the northern cliffs of Dinas Island, passing the spectacular bird-nested stack of Needle Rock. After enjoying summit views, the way drops to Pwllgwaelod where there is a fine beach and a welcoming pub. The return is across the low-lying 'neck' of the headland to the car park.

Almost an island

Dinas Island is actually part of the mainland, but only just, being almost separated at the end of the last Ice Age by meltwater flooding from a glacial lake in the Preseli Hills. Cwm Dewi is barely above sea level and the sluggish stream along its flat bottom supports luxuriant, wet woodland.

In contrast, the high cliffs of the 'island' and soaring stack of Needle Rock attract breeding guillemots and razorbills, while the western coves shelter breeding seals. On a clear day the summit view is exceptional, encompassing both Snowdon and the Wicklow Mountains — the latter 90 miles away, across the Irish Sea.

Needle Rock

Pair of guillemots

The Walk

1. Leaving the car park in **Cwm-yr-Eglwys**, follow the lane left to the **ruined church** that gave the place its name.

The original chapel was reputedly founded by St Brynach, a 6th-century Irish monk . The present church dates from the 12th century, but was partly destroyed in two great storms of 1850 and 1859. Further damage occurred in 1979 and only the west wall and belfry remain standing.

The track to the right leads to the shore, but the onward route winds left past cottages. Just before drive gates, turn off right over a **wooden bridge** and up a stepped path into the trees above the bay. After a short pull there is a fine view before resuming the climb onto the headland.

2. A gate opens onto the **National Trust's Pen Dinas estate**, the open hillside revealing a superb prospect past Newport to Cemaes Head. Inland is Mynydd Carningli, which culminates in a ragged tor at its eastern end.

Keep ahead at a fork, shortly passing above the impressive **Needle Rock**. The path then turns more steeply uphill, soon rejoining the higher path to pass through a kissing gate. Keep going, steadily rising to the trig column surmounting **Pen y Fan**. The climb is well-rewarded with a view opening west across Fishguard Bay to Strumble Head.

3. The ongoing path descends above the western cliffs and inlets of **Dinas Island**, eventually dropping to the bend of a farm track. Follow it downhill to **Pwllgwaelod** where there is an old **lime kiln** by the car park.

Yellow, green, blue: *Looking towards Pwllgwaelod from the cliffs on Dinas Head*

Before returning to Cwm-yr-Eglwys, you might want to visit the **pub** or spend time on the beach.

4. The way back lies along a metalled path signed to 'Cwm-yr-Eglwys', which runs left from the bottom of the track behind the pub. It follows the edge of a marshy, **wooded vale** across the neck of low ground connecting the 'island' to the rest of Wales. Rich in flowers and shrubs, the woodland attracts small birds and butterflies and is a relaxing finale to an invigorating walk. At the end of the path keep ahead past a small caravan site back to the car park, to complete the walk. ♦

Noisy auks on Needle Rock

In early summer the rock teems with breeding guillemots and razorbills, which otherwise spend their lives at sea, where they are expert swimmers and divers. Both auks, their black and white plumage is superficially similar, but guillemots are slightly larger and have sharp, dagger-like beaks. Nesting on ledges, they quarrel for space until, when around 20 days old, the still-flightless chicks jump into the water.

Heather and gorse frame the view across Anglas Bay towards Y Penrhyn

Goodwick & Carregwastad

Visit the site of the last invasion of Britain, passing Neolithic burial chambers and a Welsh 'Giant's Causeway'

What to expect:
Rugged clifftop paths, quiet lanes and tracks

Distance/time: 10.5km/ 6½ miles. Allow 2½ to 3 hours

Start: Car park behind Harbour Village, Goodwick

Grid ref: SM 947 389

Ordnance Survey Map: OS Explorer OL35 (North Pembrokeshire)

After the walk: The Farmhouse Kitchen café, Goodwick Square, Goodwick SA64 0BP | 07779 756838

Walk outline

Tracks and lanes take the walk from Harbour Village to tiny Llanwnda, beyond which field paths lead to the coast above Aber Felin. The route then dips with the Wales Coast Path through Cwm Felin onto Carregwastad Point. The return is along the rugged northern coast back to Goodwick, detouring out to Pen Anglas where basalt columns rise from the waves.

The Last Invasion

As the French Revolution took hold, so their foreign ambitions grew. In 1797, the French dispatched forces to foment unrest and civil war in Ireland and Britain. But bad weather decimated the armada and only one contingent, under the command of the ageing Colonel William Tate, made landfall. Composed largely of ex-convicts, his ill disciplined band came ashore near Carregwastad Point and immediately began ransacking local settlements. Finding wine from a plundered wreck, they were soon drunk. When faced with a small band of local militia they surrendered, one group giving themselves up to 47-year-old Jemima Nicholas, a pitchfork-wielding cobbler's wife.

Goodwick harbour

Stonechat

The Walk

1. Before starting the walk, have a look
at the **cromlechs** behind the village.
Walk to the back of the car park and
follow a rough path behind the houses.

*High on the hillside overlooking Goodwick,
Harbour Village was built at the beginning
of the 20th century as company housing
for employees of the newly opened ocean
terminal below. Unfortunately the houses
all but obliterated a Neolithic burial
ground and only three small cromlechs
remain of the original ten. Curiously, three
more cromlechs are spaced at intervals
to the west on virtually the same line, the
second being just off the walk at Pen-rhiw.*

Return through the car park and
take a track to the right. Keep left at
a fork towards **Pen-rhiw**, passing an
information board commemorating
the first flight across the Irish Sea in April
1912.

*After a troubled start from Hendon five
days earlier, Denys Corbet Wilson took off
in his Bleriot XI from a field near Harbour
Village on the final leg of an attempt to
reach Ireland. The flight over the Irish Sea
took 100 minutes and, although it ended
in a crash landing near Enniscorthy, Wilson
was unscathed and was the first pilot to
make the crossing.*

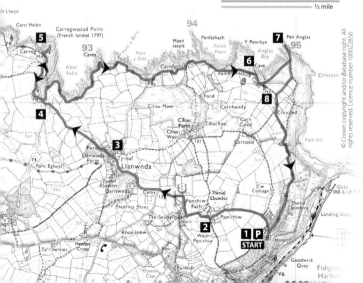

French folly: *The 'Invasion Stone' marks the landing place of French troops in 1797*

Approaching the farm, leave the track and go right to a stile beside a gate. Ahead, in the middle of the field is another **cromlech**. Walk back to the track and follow it through **Pen-rhiw farmyard**.

2. Beyond a gate at the far side, go left and then through the first gate on the right along a winding track between the fields. Keep right at a junction, soon emerging by stables. The ongoing gravel track leads to a junction by a **cemetery**.

Take the narrow lane opposite to **Llanwnda**.

3. Reaching the hamlet, walk forward at the junction past the **church** and **Gwyndaf Cottage**, home to an environment project. At the bottom of the track, go left behind a cottage and take the next right. Entering a field, cross to a gateway at the bottom and carry on along a banked track. In the next field, follow the right hedge. Carry on beyond its corner to a stile beside a gate in the bottom boundary.

4. Meeting the **Wales Coast Path**,

Geological marvel: *4, 5 and 6 sided basalt columns of dolerite exposed at Pen Anglas*

follow it forward, descending steeply into a **wooded valley**. Over a bubbling stream, climb through trees onto the headland and walk on to the **Invasion Stone**, placed in 1897 to mark the centenary of the ill-fated French landing.

5. Retrace your steps across the headland and through the valley to Point **4** on the map. This time, remain with the Coast Path above a series of tiny coves footing precipitous cliffs, the long finger of **Penfathach** eventually coming into view.

Beyond it, the path leads behind **Porth Maen**, past the broader headland of **Y Penrhyn** and then **Anglas Bay**.

6. Passing through a gate onto the **National Trust Pen Anglas estate**, branch off left along a narrower trod that winds down the hillside above the coast. Reaching a junction by a concrete stump, go left onto **Pen Anglas**. A small building straddles the neck of the promontory and care is needed if you pass around it onto the tapering point of **4, 5, and 6-sided basalt columns**.

7. Return to the junction by the concrete stump, but this time take the forward path, climbing through heather

and bracken. Bear right past a couple of enclosed fields and keep ahead over a crossing track, paths converging to the start of a track.

8. Walk ahead along the banked track. At the top, swing left in front of a gate and carry on to a kissing gate. Climbing beyond, the houses of **Harbour Village** soon appear. Eventually joining the end of a street, follow it down through the village, going right at the bottom back to the car park to complete the walk. ♦

Fishguard Harbour

In 1846, the Irish famine halted plans to develop the small fishing village into a port. Fifty or so years later the scheme was revived. The Great Western Railway was extended and 1.6 million tons of rock hewn from the hillside to create a ½-mile breakwater. For a while ocean liners such as the Lucetania and the Mauretania called, but a silting harbour soon prevented them berthing. The Atlantic trade moved to Liverpool and from 1918 only Irish traffic remained.

Strumble Head lighthouse overlooks tiny Carreg Onnen

Strumble Head

A walk around Strumble Head, one of the prime locations along the North Pembrokeshire coast for sea life watching

Distance/time: 10km/ 6¼ miles. Allow 3 to 3½ hours

Start: Coastal car park, Strumble Head

Grid ref: SM 894 412

Ordnance Survey Map: OS Explorer OL35 (North Pembrokeshire)

After the walk: The Farmhouse Kitchen café, Goodwick Square, Goodwick SA64 0BP | 07779 756838

Walk outline

After walking along the northern cliffs to Porthyschan, the route winds inland on farm tracks and lanes to climb the twin highpoints of Garn Fechan and Garn Fawr. There's a steep descent off the hill's western flank to the coast at Pwll Deri, where a short detour onto Ynys Melyn reveals 'hidden' bays in which seals often congregate. Following the coastal path back to Strumble Head, each twist and turn adds a new perspective to the view, which culminates across Carreg Onnen Bay to the lighthouse.

Strumble Head lighthouse

Strumble Head's wildlife

A pair of binoculars is a must on this walk, for it is not only seals that swim off the coast. Dolphins, porpoises and other cetaceans (or whales to you and me) pass by or come to feed and there's usually birds aplenty too. A wartime bunker perched on the cliffs near the car park has been restored as a sea-life lookout. Underfoot, the coastal turf comes alive in late spring with wildflowers. Squill, thrift, white campion, violet, kidney vetch and sea aster are just a few of the plants you will come across. And, in late summer many of the inaccessible bays below the path become nurseries for baby seals.

Atlantic grey seal and pup

The Walk

1. Before starting the walk, wander below the car park for a view of the **Strumble Head lighthouse** on **Ynys Meicel**. Also head out to the wartime **coastal lookout** below the lay-by, where displays illustrate some of the wildlife you may see.

The North Pembrokeshire coast is notoriously dangerous for shipping and in the 19th century alone, more than 60 ships were lost off Pen Caer. With the newly-built Fishguard Harbour attracting even more traffic, Trinity House commissioned a light on Ynys Meicel. Although barely separate from the mainland, it could be cut off in bad weather and was considered an off-shore light. Set 45 metres above the sea, the light flashes four times a minute and is visible for 26 nautical miles. Originally powered by oil, it was electrified in 1965 and subsequently automated.

Now follow the lane east from the car park, leaving on a sharp right bend to join the **Wales Coast Path**. Ahead, beyond Dinas Island, is distant Cemaes Head, the most northerly point of the Pembrokeshire Coast Path before it drops to St Dogmael's on the Cardigan estuary. The trail carries on above a couple of inaccessible bays before falling to a cross-path at the head of **Porthsychan**.

See forever: *Looking down from Garn Fawr to the Youth Hostel above Pwll Deri*

2. The path left drops to the bay, where low tide reveals a small beach. The route, however, lies to the right. Climb along the valley to a gate and track at the top. Go right to a farm, swinging left in front of the **farmhouse** to emerge onto a lane at **Tresinwen**.

3. Turn left and follow the lane up to a T-junction. Go right towards **St Nicholas**, the climb shortly steepening past the farm at **Caerlem**. Carry on for

another 500 metres to find a bridletrack signed off to the left.

4. Follow the track for 200 metres, looking for a stile on the right. A path leads back above the wall before turning away up towards **Garn Fechan**. Passing through the rubble of an **Iron Age embankment**, continue over the top. Drop to a stile beyond, from which a path leads right back to the lane.

The summits of both Garn Fechan and Garn Fawr are surrounded by massive earth and rubble ramparts, vivid examples of Iron Age defensive settlements. The outer

Sea girt: *Strumble Head lighthouse dominates the offshore island of Ynys Meicel*

dry-stone walls are probably contemporary and enclose small fields that extend east along the hill towards Y Garn.

5. Cross to a small car park opposite, where a path winds up onto **Garn Fawr**. Perched on an outcrop is an Ordnance Survey **'trig' column** and a **wartime observation post.** The summit views are outstanding and stretch from St David's to Cemaes Head, encompassing nearly one quarter of the Pembrokeshire coast.

6. The ongoing path drops steeply down the western flank of the hill. Near the bottom, keep ahead towards cottages, leaving the hillside over a stile. Go left to a drive and then right past **Swyn Y Morloi** to a lane.

7. Cross to the entrance of **Pwll Deri Youth Hostel** opposite, but immediately bear off right with the Coast Path. Through a gate, continue down towards the coast, a path leaving at the bottom across a narrow neck of land onto **Dinas Mawr**, which is a great place to look for seals in late summer. The main path continues around the coast, sweeping behind **Porth Maenmelyn** and onto the higher ground beyond, where there is another **wartime bunker**.

8. Beyond a **cairn** marking another superb vantage point, the path dips and weaves with the Strumble Head lighthouse intermittently appearing ahead. Shortly after crossing a marshy stream above **Pwll Arian**, the walk enters its final stage behind a delightful bay overlooked by three islands: **Ynys Onnen**, tiny **Carreg Onnen** and **Ynys Meicel** — on which the **Strumble Lighthouse** stands. Carry on back to the car park to complete the walk. ♦

Cetaceans and sunfish

Both dolphins and porpoises can be seen off Strumble Head at any time of year. Porpoises are more compact than dolphins, with a shorter snout and straight dorsal fin. On rare occasions you might even spot a minke or fin whale. During August and September, sunfish are sometimes seen off the coast. A strange-looking creature, rather flattened and seemingly all head and tail, it is the world's largest bony fish and can weigh almost a tonne.

The coast path heads out along the cliffs from Abercastle

Abercastle & Aberdraw

A captivating walk with reminders of old industry, an Iron Age promontory fort and an impressive Neolithic cromlech

What to expect:
Rugged clifftop paths with several ups and downs, a quiet lane

Distance/time: 7.5km/4¾ miles. Allow 2 to 2½ hours

Start: Small car park behind beach at Abercastle

Grid ref: SM 852 336

Ordnance Survey Map: OS Explorer OL35 (North Pembrokeshire)

After the walk: The Ship Inn, Fford y Felin, Trefin SA62 5AX | 01348 831445, OR Mill Café, Ffordd y Felin, Trefin SA62 5AX | 01348 831650

Walk outline

The outward leg climbs from Abercastle's beach past the Carreg Samson cromlech. Picking up a lane, it continues to Trefin, dropping through the village to regain the coast by a ruined corn mill above Aberdraw. Now following the Coast Path, the way returns above a series of westerly-facing bays, passing a small slate mine and an Iron Age promontory fort before rounding the headland back to Abercastle.

Abercastle

Legend surrounds many of the landmarks along Pembrokeshire's coast and such stories perpetuate memories of a distant past. It was an age when religious mystics and teachers were credited with miraculous powers in an attempt to explain the inexplicable. The striking dolmen on the hill above Abercastle was already 3,000 years old when Samson might have passed by, a 5th-century Welsh priest who went on to found a monastery at Dol in Brittany. While no ordinary man could have lifted such a massive capstone, the sainted Samson supposedly moved it using just a single finger. That finger is said to be buried on Ynys y Castell, the small islet at the mouth of Abercastle's inlet, the site of an early Christian shrine.

Mill ruins at Trefin

Chough

The Walk

1. The **Wales Coast Path** to the west leaves **Abercastle** though a gate beside the slipway, heading away beside the bay. After crossing a stream from Cwm Badau at the mouth of the natural harbour, climb briefly before leaving through a gate on the left. Follow a rising path along the fold, continuing through a gate on a concrete track past **Carreg Samson** to **Longhouse Farm**. Swing left out to a lane.

2. Turn right and follow the lane for almost 1 kilometre to **Trefin**. Keep ahead past a junction, staying with the main lane through the village and passing the **Ship Inn** at the far end. Continue downhill to a bridge above the tiny cove of **Aber Draw**.

3. On the far bank is the **ruin of a small mill**. *Cascading from the hinterland down narrow valleys to the sea, Pembrokeshire's streams gained an energy that could be tamed for work. Melin Trefin is one of many small corn mills once scattered around the coast,*

which were used to grind wheat, barley and oats that could then be shipped directly to the market ports. Built around the beginning of the 15th century, Melin Trefin was in use until 1918, inspiring the celebrated bard and Archdruid William 'Crwys' Williams to write one of the most famous poems in the Welsh language.

After looking around, return across the bridge and swing off left with the Coast Path above the stream. The cliffs here are formed of slate and the **ruined buildings** passed as the path climbs were part of a quarry.

4. The way winds on above a succession of dramatic bays and headlands, the inaccessibility of the coves attracting seals ashore in late summer to give birth to their pups.

Cliff path: *Heading back into Abercastle on the undulating Wales Coast Path*

5. After some 2.5 kilometres the path reaches **Pen Castell-coch**, where a double-banked **Iron Age defence** runs across the narrow neck of the headland. Farther on, erosion has cut through a protruding promontory to isolate its tip as an island, **Ynys Deullyn**, the tilting strata leaving a knife-edge arête along its spine.

6. Turning the point, the path wanders above a final run of cliffs before losing height to **Cwm Badau**, where across the mouth of the inlet is another detached headland, **Ynys y Castell**. Rejoin your outward steps back to the car park at **Abercastle** to complete the walk. ♦

Carreg Samson
Around 5,000 years old, the impressive stones of Carreg Samson formed the heart of a Neolithic chambered tomb. Originally covered by a large mound of stones and earth, it would have been entered through a ceremonial doorway and dark passage. The monument probably served as a communal or religious focus as well as a place of ritual burial, and excavations in 1968 revealed pottery, flints and cremated human bones.

The atmospheric ruins and sheltered harbour at Porthgain

Porthgain & Abereiddy

Superb sandy beaches, old quarries and a once-bustling harbour feature on this magnificent stretch of coast

What to expect:
Rugged clifftop paths, several ups and downs, field paths and tracks along the inland section

Distance/time: 7km/ 4¼ miles. Allow 2 to 2½ hours

Start: Car park at Porthgain

Grid ref: SM 814 324

Ordnance Survey Map: OS Explorer OL35 (North Pembrokeshire)

After the walk: The Sloop Inn, Porthgain SA62 5BN | 01348 831449

Walk outline

Field paths and tracks take the outward leg across Ynys Barry, an island in name only with streams defining its inland flanks. At Abereiddy, the beach, ruins and old quarry workings are great to explore before heading back along the coast path. There's another superb beach at Traeth Llyfn and then more quarries, old buildings and the trough of an inclined tramway to ponder before descending a steep flight of steps back to Porthgain harbour.

The demands of industry

Until the 19th century, the sheltered inlet of Porthgain was a quiet fishing village and the headlands either side managed for farming and grazing. All that changed with the sudden growth of manufacturing industry across Britain, which created an unprecedented demand for materials to build new factories and ports, houses for workers and the canals, railways and roads to connect them all together. Although the outcrops of slate here were not of the best quality, they were easily quarried and could be shipped directly to the rapidly growing conurbations around Britain. The harbour and enigmatic ruins of Porthgain and Abereiddy represented a huge investment, yet the industrial adventure was over and done within 80 years.

Coastal marker, Porthgain

Fulmar

Safe haven: *Local fishing boats moored behind the stout harbour wall at Porthgain*

The Walk

1. Walk away from **Porthgain harbour**, keeping right of the **old brick works**. Just past a telephone box, bear off left on a track. After 50 metres, at a fingerpost, leave over a **footbridge** on the right. Swing left beside a stream and through a gate. Continue up the left edge of a couple of fields, crossing the corner of a third, smaller enclosure to emerge onto a track by **Felindre House**.

2. Go right but then leave after a few steps through a gate. Head away to a stile in the far left corner and maintain the same heading across the next field, dropping out over a stile onto a lane.

3. Go left and immediately bear right along a track, curving right past a fork to **Ynys Barry Farm**. Keep ahead between the buildings and on over the crest of a hill. At the track's end, go over a stile by the lefthand of two gates. Walk away beside the left hedge, swinging right within the bottom corner to a gate and stile. Slant ahead across the valley side to leave by a **toilet block**. Walk out past a row of **ruined cottages** to a car park behind **Abereiddy beach**.

4. The way back leaves up steps by the ruined cottages. At the top, go left past a round slate building, the quarry's **old powder store**.

The opening of Ynys Barry's slate quarries around 1840 drew workers from miles around, some walking to work from as far away as St David's. Unsuited for roofing slates, the stone was cut as slabs for lintels, steps, kerbs and mantlepieces. Yet despite huge investment — the construction of the harbour and a tramway from the workings at Abereiddy in 1851 and later, a tunnel from the base of the Porthgain quarry pit direct to the harbour — the quarries rarely proved profitable and were closed more than once because of bankruptcy.

Through a gate, the **Wales Coast Path** branches off right, but first keep ahead to the **Blue Lagoon**.

5. Return to the gate and follow the Coast Path left, winding above the lagoon and past the partially isolated promontory of **Trwyncastell** with its **ruined tower**. The way continues above cliffs before turning north behind **Traeth Llyfn**. Just before a gate above the far end of the bay, a flight of metal steps leads down to the beach.

6. The path winds on above **Porth Egr**

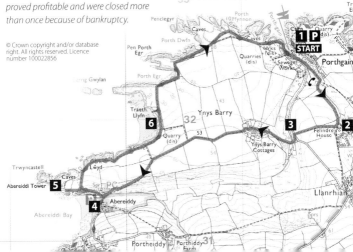

Out on a limb: *Enigmatic Abereiddy Tower perches on the rocky tip of Trwyncastell*

and **Porth Dwfn** before reaching the first of the massive **Porthgain quarries**.

Until the invention of dynamite by Alfred Nobel in 1867, quarrying and tunnelling through very hard rock was almost impossible. The new explosive, however, enabled the exploitation of an outcrop of dolerite just west of Porthgain, which was sold as road-stone. The quarry opened in 1889, the crushed rock being stored in massive hoppers beside the harbour prior to being loaded onto ships for export as far away as London and Ireland. However, the introduction of rubber-tyred vehicles and tar-sealed roads eventually killed the trade and the quarry closed in 1931.

Towards the far end, you can walk back along the incline to the large road-stone quarry, where several buildings remain. A little farther on are more workings, while over to the right is the deep pit of the original slate quarry. The route, however, keeps roughly ahead with the Coast Path, losing height and then descending steps to a cottage, once the **Harbour Pilot's office**.

In 1889, in an effort to increase the profitability of the slate workings a large brickworks and kiln were constructed

behind the harbour to utilise the crushed waste from the quarries. The new enterprise helped revive the industry for a while but the tramway from Abereiddy finally closed in 1906, with brick exports ending six years later. The derelict brickworks have since been restored and now house a restaurant.

Head back along the **quayside** to the car park to complete the walk. ♦

'Blue Lagoon'

The row of ruined cottages behind the beach are all that remain of the small settlement that sprang up beside Abereiddy's slate quarry. The workings operated for around half a century and were subsequently flooded to create a harbour. Now know as the Blue Lagoon because of the tinted water caused by mineral seepage from the rocks, the deep pool has become a favourite location for coasteering, underwater diving and cliff diving.

Welsh ponies grazing alongside the Wales Coast Path on St David's Head

St David's Head

An impressive walk with Neolithic burials, a prehistoric village and a glimpse of Ireland from Carn Llidi

What to expect:
A maze of paths on the headland. Easy scrambling to the rocky top of Carn Llidi

Distance/time: 7km/ 4½miles. Allow 2 to 2½ hours

Start: Car park at Whitesands Bay (charge)

Grid ref: SM 733 271

Ordnance Survey Map: OS Explorer OL35 (North Pembrokeshire)

After the walk: Whitesands Beach Café, St Davids SA62 6PS | 01437 720168, OR Old Cross Hotel, Cross Square, St David's SA62 6SP | 01437 720394

Walk outline

Beginning from the popular sandy beach at Whitesands Bay, the walk winds up across coastal moor onto the rocky summit of Carn Llidi. Dropping back to the coast, the route continues above sheer cliffs onto St David's Head before returning behind the smaller bays of Porthmelgan and Porth Lleuog.

St David's Head and Carn Llidi

On a clear day you can see Ireland from the summit of Carn Llidi, a sight that might have inspired St Patrick's vision to convert the island to Christianity.

Natural rock arch

But even in the 5th century, this place was already ancient. On the walk towards the headland, lookout for the silhouette of Coetan Arthur, the remains of a Neolithic burial chamber, perhaps 6,000 years old. There are more cromlechs near the top of Carn Llidi, below which it is possible to make out field patterns laid out by farmers during the late Bronze Age. Across the tip of the peninsula is a stone rampart, built to defend an Iron Age settlement whose hut foundations can still be seen amongst the rocks.

St David's Head ponies

The Walk

Whitesands Bay is justly named. The expansive sweep of sparkling sand is one of the finest in the country. Because it faces the prevailing Atlantic winds, it can experience massive waves — making it a prime venue for surfers. For those in search of a more secluded location, the two smaller bays of Porth Lleuog and Porthmelgan are sheltered between intriguing outcrops. Very low tides can expose the remnants of a forest anciently flooded by a rising sea, with trees such as hazel, oak and pine being identified. Animal bones have also been discovered, revealing that red deer, wild cattle and bears once roamed the area.

1. The **Wales Coast Path** leaves the car park by a telephone box, running beside

rough grass hiding the **site of a Celtic chapel built to St Patrick**.

Whitesands Bay is one of the traditional places from which Patrick embarked upon his conversion of Ireland. The beach became a landing for both pilgrims and traders crossing the Irish Sea and a small chapel was erected, the site marked today by a plaque just north of the car park. It is possible that there was a Bronze Age trade in copper and gold from the Wicklow Hills, taken inland along an ancient track over the Preseli Hills. Some archaeologists believe that the bay is also the site of a

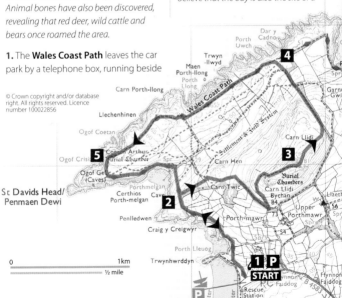

Island fling: *Looking out to sea beyond Carn Llidi with Ramsey Island on the horizon*

Roman port and that the dunes conceal an early Christian settlement founded by St David before he moved to the more sheltered site in the Alun valley where St David's Cathedral now stands.

Keep right with the main path above **Porth Lleuog**.

2. Through a gate, the path fragments. Keep right and take the first right, which climbs gently towards **Carn Llidi**. Bear right as a second path joins, the way shortly curving over the western shoulder of the hill. Dropping to a junction, double back sharp left, climbing again to reach the ruin of a **wartime lookout**, near which are the **remains of Neolithic cromlechs**. Continue on a fainter path to a small platform beneath the summit, from which it is an easy scramble to the top.

3. Drop back to find a path off to the right that picks its way across the north-western slope of the ridge. Approaching the far end of the rocky outcrop, the path loses height, heading towards a

Sacred site?: *The Coetan Arthur cromlech on St David's Head overlooks Ramsey Island*

wall where it meets a path crossing the hill's north eastern shoulder. Follow it left, descending towards the coast. At a fork near the corner of a wall, bear left to a crossing of paths.

4. Go forward, rising to meet the Coast Path. Follow it left, maintaining the high ground towards St David's Head. Reaching a junction of paths, bear right to climb through an **Iron Age embankment**. Walk on above the cliffs, sticking with the main path. Just beyond a rocky outcrop, keep a lookout over to

the left for the fine burial chamber of **Coetan Arthur** (SM 725 280).

Dramatically situated on a ridge above St David's Head, Coetan Arthur, or 'Arthur's Quoit', is all that remains of a Neolithic passage grave dating from around 3,000 BC. Now partially collapsed, the burial chamber features a massive capstone supported by one large upright. In prehistoric times the tomb would have been covered by a long mound of earth and stones.

Return to the main path and carry on across a **second embankment wall**, some 50 metres after which there are a

number of **hut circles**. Continue onto the narrowing tip of the headland for the views to Ramsey and the outlying islands.

5. Retrace your steps past the hut circles and through the defensive wall. Now, keep to the right path, which gently falls across the hillside above **Porthmelgan**. Just beyond the head of the bay, turn right, cross a stream and follow the main path back to the car park to complete the walk. ♦

Rare birds?

The conspicuously red beaked and booted chough is Britain's scarcest crow, nesting on cliffs and foraging for insects on coastal pastures. They are readily identified by their noisy 'chee-ow' call and superbly acrobatic flight. On the gorse heaths you might also spot a Dartford warbler, which, although more usually found in southern England, have recently taken advantage of mild winters to extend their range to Pembrokeshire.

The distinctive rocky outcrop of Carn Llidi seen from the southern end of Whitesands Bay

St David's peninsula

A grand stretch of cliffs overlooking Ramsey Sound to one of Pembrokeshire's largest offshore island nature reserves

What to expect:
Country lanes and tracks with rugged, undulating clifftop coast path

Distance/time: 13.5km/ 8½ miles. Allow 3½ to 4 hours

Start: National Trust car park at Porth Clais (pay and display)

Grid ref: SM 740 242

Ordnance Survey Map: OS Explorer OL35 (North Pembrokeshire)

After the walk: The Kiosk, National Trust car park, Porth Clais OR The Bishops, Cross Square, St David's SA62 6SL | 01437 720422

Walk outline

The walk sets off along inland lanes, ultimately following a track to the coast at Whitesands Bay. After passing behind the secluded sandy beach of Porthselau, the way follows the coastal cliffs above Ramsey Sound. After turning the point, the path eventually drops to the beach at Porthlysgi Bay. Returning to high ground above Carreg Frân, there is a final run of cliffs before turning into the sheltered inlet of Porth Clais.

Pen Dal-aderyn

Befittingly, the western tip of mainland Wales is a rugged but hauntingly beautiful spot, a wild coast of low jagged cliffs that overlooks a turbulent stretch of water between it and Ramsey Island. Tides race through the narrow channel of Ramsey Sound, concentrating shoals of fish that bring porpoises and seals to feed.

Pen Dal-aderyn, translated as the 'headland of birds', is aptly named for the number of seabirds that wheel and swoop over the waves, whilst Ramsey Island is one of the largest bird reserves on the coast, and can be visited by boat from nearby St Justinian.

Lifeboat station, Porthstinian

Peregrine pair

The Walk

1. Out of the car park, turn right up the lane, later going forward at a crossroads towards 'St Justinian'. Reaching a T-junction, walk left and then, after 300 metres, fork right to **Treleddyn**. Carry on ahead between the buildings, bearing right at the far end on a hedge-banked track signed as a bridleway. After 800 metres, as the way once more becomes metalled, leave along a track off to the left. It shortly bends right as the **Wales Coast Path** joins from the left.

2. To reach **Whitesands beach** (Point **3** on the map), walk a short distance to the right before branching off left opposite **'The Cabin'.** A path runs through the dunes to the **car park and café** behind the beach.

The way back, however, is to the left along the Coast Path. After winding behind the sheltered bay of **Porthselau** (where you can reach the sand) the path continues onto the headland above a succession of rocky coves. Rounding **Point St John**, the view opens across Ramsey Sound to Ramsey Island.

Tides can race through Ramsey Sound at up to six knots, creating an obvious 'cascade' as they surge over The Bitches, a notorious reef of rocks towards the Ramsey Island shore. In addition to the regular appearance of seals and porpoises, there

Sound and fury: *The tide rips through The Bitches reef on the far side of Ramsey Sound*

are occasional sightings of dolphins. Birds to look out for include choughs (looking rather like a crow but with red bill and legs) and peregrine falcons, which nest on Ramsey's high cliffs. During the summer, there is a ferry to the island or you can take an exciting RIB trip through Ramsey Sound and below the western cliffs, where there are dark sea caves. Bookings should be made in advance in St David's.

The path eventually turns in above **Porthstinian** from which boats to Ramsey embark. Nearby are the remains of **St Justinian's Chapel**.

St Justian so impressed St David with his piety that he became his confessor and was made abbot of the monastery. However, he was critical of the monks' lax behaviour and soon retreated to Ramsey Island as a hermit. His austere demands angered some and he was brutally murdered. Legend has it that he walked back across the sound carrying his severed head to be buried where the chapel at St Justinian now stands. His remains were later reinterred in St David's Cathedral.

Sheltering arm: *A sturdy harbour wall protects the narrow inlet at Porth Clais*

4. The path passes behind the cable winch and steps down to the lifeboat station to carry on above the sound. Farther on, after twisting around **Carn ar Wig**, the path follows the western-most stretch of the St David's peninsula, passing the fenced shaft of an **abandoned copper mine** at **Penmaenmelyn**.

The intriguing shaft is all that remains of the Treginnis copper mine. Sporadic outcrops of copper ore occur along the coast and have been worked for centuries, notably a vein to the east near Dinas Fawr. The Treginnis mine was begun in 1827, but failed to produce a significant return and closed only nine years later.

5. Continuing beyond the mine around the point, the path passes above more tiny coves and fractured rocks. Keep an eye open for seals and porpoises, which feed in the area. The path eventually winds in above **Porthlysgi Bay**, dropping to the shore at its head. It is a wonderfully sheltered bay that catches the afternoon sun. If you venture into the smaller cove at the far side, keep an eye on the tide, which cuts it off from the main beach with no other way out.

6. The ongoing path climbs back onto the cliffs, winding around a final point before eventually turning in above the narrow inlet of **Porth Clais**. The path runs high above the harbour wall that protects the entrance, gently losing height to a **wharf** where a group of well-preserved **lime kilns** stand. Emerging onto the lane, go left back to the car park to complete the walk. ♦

Porth Clais

The Porth Clais inlet is typical of many along the coast, the result of a post-glacial stream gouging a deep valley. Subsequently flooded by rising sea levels, it later became a haven used by the Romans. It was the medieval port for St David's, bringing in limestone and coal for burning in quayside kilns to make fertiliser for the fields. More recently, coal was brought in for a gasworks that supplied St David's, the site now occupied by the car park.

St David's Cathedral was originally built in a valley to hide it from Viking raiders

St David's & St Non's

Britain's smallest city, St David's birthplace and the spring where he was baptised feature in this superb coastal walk

What to expect:
Field trods, rugged cliff paths and surfaced streets in St David's

Distance/time: 7km/ 4½ miles. Allow 1½ to 2 hours

Start: Oriel Y Parc, St David's (pay and display)

Grid ref: SM 757 251

Ordnance Survey Map: OS Explorer OL35 (North Pembrokeshire)

After the walk: Oriel Y Parc Café, National Park Visitor Centre, St David's SA62 6NW | 01437 721512, OR The Old Cross Hotel, Cross Square, St David's SA62 6SP | 01437 720387

Walk outline
From the car park, the route soon leaves the outskirts of St David's crossing fields to meet the coast at St Non's. The walk continues above coastal cliffs before turning in above the deep inlet of Porth Clais. After returning across the fields, the final section winds through the old city past the Cathedral and Bishops' Palace before heading back along the main street back to the car park.

St David's
Cardiff might be the secular capital of Wales, but St David's is its spiritual heart, where the rocks of an ancient landscape remain a tangible link with the beginnings of Christianity in the country. Faith, fact and legend lie at the heart of a tradition of pilgrimage that stretches back almost to St David himself and, despite its modern popularity as a tourist spot, the area retains a sense of beauty and natural tranquility that can be appreciated by anyone, regardless of creed.

Coasteering near St David's

This short walk includes some of the pilgrims' stopping places and the stretch of cliff below the city is as lovely as any along the Pembrokeshire coast, where seabirds and perhaps the occasional bobbing seal might be your only company.

Atlantic grey seal

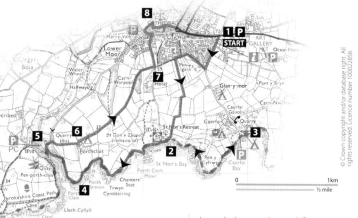

The Walk

1. Leave the car park onto **Ffordd Caerfai** and follow it left. Where the houses finish, turn right into **Maes-y-Dre**. As that then bends, bear off left along a footpath. Some 100 metres after it swings left, watch for a hedged path leaving on the left signed to 'St Non's'. Passing through gates, swing right and then left. Through more gates at the end, go right and ultimately left at the edge of a final field towards the coast. Exit through a gate at the bottom and wind out to the **Wales Coast Path** beside the **St Non's retreat**.

2. If you have time for the beach, first go left around the triangular headland of **Pen y Cyfrwy** to **Caerfai Bay**, where

the path drops to the sand (Point **3** on the map).

The ongoing route, however, lies to the right past **St Non's**, where the **tiny chapel** just above the path is always open. In the garden's south west corner is **St Non's Well**, while in a field to the west is the **ruin of St Non's church**, a 7th-century chapel built to mark the place where St David was born and set within the remnants of a **Bronze Age stone circle**.

Drop back to the Coast Path and continue to the right. There are few places along the Pembrokeshire coast where the cliff scenery is not spectacular and here is no exception. The cliffs are fractured into a never-ending succession of tiny projections and coves where

Ocean adventurers: *Sea kayakers exploring the foot of towering cliffs in St Non's Bay*

shattered rocks and the stumps of old stacks are washed by the waves. All are perches for seabirds and seals bobbing in the water are a common sight.

4. Eventually the path turns in to the deep, narrow inlet of **Porth Clais**, its mouth protected by a sturdy harbour wall offering the only all-tide moorings. Just beyond the point, a path drops to the harbour, but the Coast Path remains high above the inlet. Farther on,

however, at a fork, bear left descending above a couple of **lime kilns** to the head of the estuary and out onto a lane.

5. Across the bridge to the left, a **National Trust kiosk** by the entrance to a small car park sells cakes and drinks. Hidden in the bracken nearby is the **holy well** where St David was baptised.

The way back, however, is to the right. Leave the lane on the first left bend to climb a stepped path through thick scrub on the right. At the top, keep ahead across grazing and then at the

Important site: *The ruined medieval Bishop's Palace sits next to St David's Cathedral*

edge of a camping field to **Porthclais Farm**.

6. Entering the yard, swing left along a track, but almost immediately turn off through a gate on the right. A path leads away beside a couple of fields and then between banks for a good 800 metres. Keep ahead as another path joins from the right to emerge onto a lane by **Warpool Court Hotel**.

7. To the left, the lane leads back to **St Davids**, becoming a street as it bends past houses. Keep ahead at the first

junction and then go left. After 75 metres, opposite another junction, turn right along a metalled track towards the **Cathedral** and **Bishop's Palace**.

The original church founded by St David was destroyed in the 11th century by Viking raiders. The Cathedral was begun in 1180 and altered many times over the centuries. By the mid-19th century, however, it was neglected and Sir Gilbert Scott was commissioned to undertake a major restoration. Concealed in a hollow, the Cathedral's plain façade hides the startling beauty of its inner decoration. St David's shrine has recently been restored and its niches contain reliquaries said to

contain the remains of St David and St Justinian.

8. Having explored the ecclesiastical precincts, climb the 39 steps from the south front of the Cathedral. Turn left through an arch and follow the ongoing street into the square at the **centre of St David's.** Keep ahead along **High Street** back to the car park to complete the walk. ♦

St Non's Well

Water has a ritual significance and natural springs are often revered as symbols of vitality and rebirth. The spring at St Non's was perhaps sacred to the builders of the nearby Bronze Age stone circle. It was later adopted as a holy well by Celtic Christians, who claimed the water appeared upon the birth of St David. The well's waters were used both for baptism and healing, drawing pilgrims suffering from rheumatism and eye disease.

The sheltered harbour at Solva occupies a flooded post-glacial stream valley

Solva

An attractive harbour, prehistoric cromlechs and a stunning coastline are among the highlights of this exhilarating walk

What to expect:
Field trods and a rugged coastal path with some steep climbs and descents

Distance/time: 8km/ 5 miles. Allow 2 to 2½ hours

Start: Quayside car park at Solva (pay and display)

Grid ref: SM 805 242

Ordnance Survey Map: OS Explorer OL35 (North Pembrokeshire)

After the walk: The Harbour Inn, Main Street, Solva SA62 6UT | 01437 720013

Walk outline

After climbing above the Solva inlet over Gribin to the tiny cove of Gwadn, the route takes to the fields past St Elvis and Lochvane farms to the coast above Porthmynawyd. The undulating return along the cliff path passes the dramatic rocky promontories of Dinas Fach and Dinas Fawr before curving above inaccessible bays back to Gwadn. There is a final steep climb back over Gribin before returning to Solva Harbour

Solva's rich history

Hidden from the sea by a long inlet and projecting headlands, Solva's harbour is the most sheltered haven within the sweep of St Bride's Bay. The high promontory of the Gribin overlooking its mouth was the site of an Iron Age fort and, during the Middle Ages, Solva developed as the main trading port along this part of coast. One of the main imports was limestone, which was roasted in the several lime kilns surrounding the harbour before being carted inland to fertilise the fields. Just to the east, around Dinas Fawr, outcropping copper and lead ores were mined from at least the 16th century, while inland at St Elvis Farm is a cromlech and the remains of a holy well and church.

Cromlech, St Elvis Farm

Gannet

The Walk

1. Leave the back of the car park by the **Harbour Inn** to cross a bridge over the **River Solva**.

In its heyday, more than 30 trading ships were operating out of Solva, bringing in coal, limestone and other commodities for the small community in exchange for corn, woollen cloth and other local produce. Fishing was an important industry too, but many folk supplemented their diet by foraging along the cliffs for seabirds and their eggs. Also found amongst the rocks is samphire, a squat fleshy plant that must be pickled or cooked as a vegetable. It must

have once grown here in profusion since 'Solfach' derives from the Norse name for the plant.

Go left and then sharp right to climb above the harbour along the flank of a **wooded ridge**. At the first fork, branch left and continue up through the trees to emerge on the top of the ridge. Towards the far end of the ridge, bear left with the **Wales Coast Path**, dropping steeply to the head of a small cove at **Gwadn**.

2. Cross a stream but instead of climbing away at the far side of the shingle beach with the Coast Path, turn off left along the base of the valley. After 75 metres, at

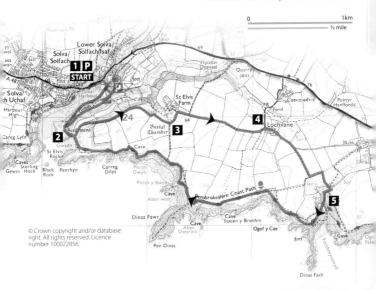

Rocky rib: *The hogsback ridge of Gribin separates Gwadn cove from Solva harbour*

a fork, branch right and climb across the hillside. At the top, curve right through a gate and continue at the edge of a couple of fields to emerge through a gate at the far end. Walk forward to a junction, passing a small enclosure on the right containing the remains of **two cromlechs**.

3. Fork left towards **St Elvis Farm**, passing through a gate on the right onto a parallel path.

St Elvis, also known as St Ailbe, was a 6th-century bishop of Munster who, according to tradition, taught and baptised St David. Although demolished in the 19th century, a holy well and chapel dedicated to St Teilo was a halting place for pilgrims on their way to St David's. Those who were sick were given holy water from the well and left to rest beside the cromlech. Sleep would bring a cure but a visitation by the raven Caldrius foretold death.

Through a gate at the end, turn right on a track towards 'Lochvane'. Where it swings left at the top, keep ahead

Ancient river valley: *Solva, Gribin and Gwadn bay from Penrhyn headland*

through a kissing gate. Continue forward at the edge of successive fields and then along a hedged track to emerge at **Lochvane**.

4. Walk on past cottages and along the lane beyond. After 400 metres, as the lane then bends left, keep ahead on another hedge-banked path. Over a stile at the end, turn left along the edge of a field, swinging right within the corner. Leave at the bottom over a stile hidden in a small copse of hazel and swing left to a junction. Go right, dropping

through thicket and across a stream to meet the Coast Path.

5. The path ahead leads down to **Porthmynawyd** — a tiny shingle-backed cove. The way back however lies to the right. Recrossing the stream, the path climbs onto the cliff and winds on above the head of **Dinas Fach**. Continue along the coast, eventually turning past the neck of the projecting finger of **Dinas Fawr.**

Carry on above **Aber-west** and **Porth y Bŵch**, both inviting bays but accessible only from the sea. Eventually, the path turns above the last promontory of

Penrhyn and **St Elvis Rock** before dropping back to Gwadn at Point **2**. Cross the back of the beach and climb steeply away, but this time, keep left at the first fork, descending along the wooded flank of the promontory

and passing a pillar commemorating the donation of the headland to the National Trust in 1937. The path emerges by **lime kilns**. Walk up to the head of the inlet, crossing the bridge back to the car park to complete the walk. ♦

Lime Kilns

Lime kilns are a feature of many of north Pembrokeshire's tiny coves; in fact just about anywhere with a track down to a safe landing may have one. Small ships carrying limestone were beached on the shore to be unloaded at low tide. The rock was burnt with coal in the kilns before being carted inland as quicklime to be spread on the fields as a 'soil sweetener' and primitive fertiliser.

Useful Information

Wales Coast Path
Comprehensive information about all sections of the Wales Coast Path can be found at www.walescoastpath.gov.uk

Visit Pembrokeshire
Pembrokeshire's official tourism website covers everything from accommodation and special events to attractions and adventure. **www.visitpembrokeshire.com**

Pembrokeshire Coast National Park
The Pembrokeshire Coast National Park website also has information on things to see and do, plus a host of practical details to help plan your visit.
www.pembrokeshirecoast.org.uk

Tourist Information Centres
The main TICs provide free information on everything from accommodation and transport to what's on and walking advice.

St David's - 01437 720392 - info@orielyparc.co.uk

Fishguard - 01348 776636 - fishguard.tic@pembrokeshire.gov.uk

Fishguard Harbour - 01348 874737

Weather
Online weather forecasts for Pembrokeshire are available from the Met Office at **www.metoffice.gov.uk**

Rail Travel
The only rail service in the area is to the Fishguard ferry port.

Information is available from National Rail Enquiries on 08457 484950 or **www.nationalrail.com.uk**

Bus Travel
A dedicated bus network serves the whole of the Coast Path, running every day during the summer months but with a limited service in winter.

Pembrokeshire Greenways - 01437 776313 - **www.pembrokeshiregreenways.co.uk/**

Traveline Cymru - 0871 200 22 33 - **www.travelinecymru.info**